SNAKES

Printed in Hong Kong

99 00 01 02 03 5 4 3 2 1

Library of Congress Cataloging-in-Publication Data
Gaywood, Martin
Snakes / Martin Gaywood and Ian Spellerberg.
p. cm. — (WorldLife library)
Includes bibliographical references.
ISBN 0-89658-449-6 (alk. paper)
I. Snakes. I. Spellerberg, Ian F. II. Title. III. Series.
QL666.06G249 1999
597.96–dc21   99-14768
                                                        CIP

Distributed in Canada by Raincoast Books, 8680 Cambie Street, Vancouver, B.C. V6P 6M9

Published by Voyageur Press, Inc.
123 North Second Street, P. O. Box 338, Stillwater, MN 55082, U.S.A.
651-430-2210, fax 651-430-2211

Educators, fundraisers, premium and gift buyers, publicists and marketing managers: Looking for creative products and new sales ideas? Voyageur Press books are available at special discounts when purchased in quantities, and special editions can be created to your specifications. For details contact the marketing department at 800-888-9653.

Acknowledgements
This book summarises the work of many professional and amateur herpetologists and we pay tribute to their efforts in helping to unlock the secrets of a very special group of animals. Many thanks also go to those who helped us in the writing of this book, in particular Des Thompson and Richard Griffiths for providing comments on draft texts, and Fiona Leslie for comments and patient encouragement.

Front cover photograph: Horned viper (*Cerastes cerastes gasparetti*)   Back cover photograph: Nelson's milk snake (*Lampropeltis triangulum nelsoni*)
Page 1 photograph: Colubrid snake (*dryocalamus tristrigatus*)   Page 4 photograph: Copperhead snake (*Agkistrod contortrix*)

Photographs copyright © 1999 by

Front cover © Xavier Eichaker (Still Pictures)
Back cover © Chris Mattison
Page 1 © Michael and Patricia Fogden
Page 4 © Chris Mattison
Page 6 © Gerry Ellis (Minden Pictures)
Page 7 © Michael and Patricia Fogden
Page 9 © John Cancalosi (Bruce Coleman Limited)
Page 10 © Chris Mattison
Page 11 © Benny Van Damme (Still Pictures)
Page 13 © Michael and Patricia Fogden
Page 14 © Michael and Patricia Fogden
Page 17 © Michael and Patricia Fogden
Page 18 © Chris Mattison
Page 21 © Michael and Patricia Fogden
Page 22 Top © Thierry Montford (Still Pictures)

Page 22 Bottom © Chris Mattison
Page 25 © Jim Brandenburgh (Minden Pictures)
Page 26 © Chris Mattison
Page 29 © Laurie Campbell
Page 31 © Chris Mattison
Page 32 © Michael and Patricia Fogden
Page 35 © Michael and Patricia Fogden
Page 36 © Mark O'Shea
Page 38 © Roland Seitre (Still Pictures)
Page 41 © Michael and Patricia Fogden
Page 42 © Mark O'Shea
Page 43 © Daniel Heuclin (NHPA)
Page 45 © Gunter Ziesler (Bruce Coleman Limited)
Page 46 © Michael and Patricia Fogden
Page 48 © Chris Mattison

Page 49 © John Cancalosi (Bruce Coleman Limited)
Page 51 © Anthony Bannister (NHPA)
Page 52 © Mark O'Shea
Page 54 © Michael and Patricia Fogden
Page 55 © Michael and Patricia Fogden
Page 57 © Chris Mattison
Page 59 © Xavier Eichaker (Still Pictures)
Page 60 © Michael and Patricia Fogden
Page 63 © Michael and Patricia Fogden
Page 65 © Michael and Patricia Fogden
Page 66 © Michael and Patricia Fogden
Page 69 © Michael and Patricia Fogden
Page 70 © Martin Gaywood

SNAKES

Martin Gaywood & Ian Spellerberg

WORLDLIFE
LIBRARY

Voyageur Press

Contents

Snakes – Some Perceptions

'I had been extolling the virtues of the three grass snakes I had in my hand when I turned to look at the young lad I was talking to. Immediately I stopped. He had turned as white as a sheet, eyes transfixed on the squirming animals, with tears trickling down his cheeks. "Don't worry, I'm putting them back in the bucket" I said, at the same time stepping back a few yards to give him a bit of space, and then making a big show of sealing the lid tight on the container. He started to dry his eyes, embarrassed at the reaction the snakes had unexpectedly provoked in him and mumbling unnecessary apologies. Yet only a few minutes earlier he had seen me arrive at the university with my bucket of newly caught study animals from the New Forest, and he was eager to see what I had. The snakes made an impressive sight since they had coiled themselves into a tangled ball, so that when I pulled them out to show him they writhed around my hand in a seething mass of green bodies, darting tongues and angry hissing. I had wrongly thought that by emphasising that they were completely harmless I would allay any fears he had.'
– From an account by Martin Gaywood while undertaking research at Southampton University.

Arizona mountain king snake.

What is it about snakes that provokes such strong reactions in people? The extreme reaction described above seems to sum up the feelings many folk have towards

The Aruba rattlesnake is currently threatened by habitat loss and by collectors in the West Indies.

snakes, a combination of fascination, interest, loathing and even fear. It is difficult to put a finger on what so many people dislike about them. It might be because they are considered slimy, unblinking, cold and heartless predators which crawl on their bellies and attack people at will; it might be a consequence of a hatred built from stories and legends which often depict snakes or serpent-like monsters as forces of evil. Yet many of these beliefs are simply untrue.

We wish this book to demonstrate the incredible diversity of snakes and to look at the remarkable ways they have evolved to survive. We hope it will appeal to snake enthusiasts, and give others a chance to find out a little more about this fascinating group of reptiles. Hopefully it will dispel some of the myths that have grown up around them. The bookshelves of shops and libraries typically heave with volumes about the furry or feathered members of the animal kingdom, but books on snakes tend to be harder to find.

There are around 2700 species of snakes in the world, each with its own unique way of surviving in its environment. They have proved remarkably successful and can be found in a wide diversity of habitats, ranging from the open sea to rivers, marshland, forests, grasslands, mountains and deserts. They occur on every continent, with the exception of Antarctica, and, despite being ectothermic (or 'cold-blooded'), some species range as far north as the Arctic Circle. They have evolved a variety of lifestyles, for example feeding on a wide range of prey species and utilising different hunting, defensive and reproductive strategies. Snakes also have a diverse range of physical features despite having a basic 'serpentine' body shape which we all find instantly recognizable.

The diversity of snakes is the main theme through this book, and we hope it will stimulate a wider appreciation of their place within the natural environment. The accompanying photographs show these animals not only as supreme predators but also as truly beautiful animals.

Parrot snake, a tropical American species which hunts for frogs in low tree branches and bushes.

What are Snakes?

Snake Relations

Snakes are reptiles, a group of vertebrate animals which are characterized by having scaly, horny skins and the ability to produce shelled eggs. All living reptiles are divided into four major groups: Squamata – snakes, lizards and amphisbaenids; Testudines – tortoises and turtles; Crocodilia – alligators and crocodiles; Rhynchocephalia – tuatara.

The snakes are therefore a sub-group (technically called Serpentes or Ophidia), within the Squamata. In addition to these reptile groups, many others, such as the dinosaurs, are now extinct.

Snakes differ from their closest relatives, the lizards, in not having any limbs or limb girdles (although some of the more primitive snakes retain vestigial hind limbs and hind-limb girdles), no movable eyelids and no external ear openings. Also, snakes usually have a deeply forked tongue, and a single row of scales on their underside. To

The adder lives as far north as the Arctic circle.

complicate matters, some lizards have no legs and are quite 'snake-like' in appearance, but they do have other lizard features such as moving eyelids. The other close relatives of the snakes, the burrowing amphisbaenids or 'worm lizards', are very snake-like in appearance since they generally have no legs and no movable eyelids. However they have certain anatomical and other characteristics which set them apart from the snakes, such as skin with grooves which separate rings of small scales.

Breeding aggregations of the red-sided garter snake can number several hundred individuals.

The Origin of Snakes

Until recently, scientific opinion favored the idea of snakes evolving from burrowing lizards. Such a lifestyle seemed to explain why ancestral lizards may have eventually lost their limbs and external ear openings through evolutionary time, as they would have been virtually useless when burrowing underground. Modern snakes lack both these features. However, as long ago as the end of the nineteenth century, scientists suggested an alternative marine origin to snakes and there is now, once again, strong support for this theory. This began in the late 1970s when a fossil of a strange animal was found in a quarry near Jerusalem. The animal was named *Pachyrachis problematicus* (literally, the 'problematic thick-ribbed animal'), and was believed to have been just under 3 ft (1 m) long, snake-like in appearance but with two small hind legs, each around 1 in (2–3 cm) in length. *Pachyrachis* lived in the prehistoric oceans 100 million years ago and had features well adapted for a marine lifestyle, such as a flattened tail for propulsion and heavy ribs to counteract the buoyancy of its lungs. It also lacked ear drums, since they would have been useless underwater, and had the characteristic limbless, elongated, snake-like body which could have helped with swimming. Perhaps *Pachyrachis* was the ancestor of modern snakes.

The Snake Families

Snakes can be sub-divided into 15 main families, although there is no agreement among biologists as to how, precisely, snakes should be classified. The incredible diversity of snakes is evident from taking a brief look at these families, starting with the more primitive, present-day ones (more details are given in the table at the back of the book).

Family Leptotyphlopidae – Thread snakes (about 60 species). These are small, slender snakes from America, Africa and western Asia. They tend to have a burrowing lifestyle and feed on invertebrates. Those species studied so far are oviparous (they lay eggs). They have vestigial pelvic girdles and hind limbs, small eyes and mouths, and polished, overlapping scales.

Western thread snake from Namibia, a member of family
Leptotyphlopidae (from the Greek leptos, meaning thin). Members of
this family are small and slender snakes which tend to have a burrowing
lifestyle and feed on invertebrates. Those species studied so far
lay eggs. Note the small eyes and polished scales.

*Giant blind snake from South Africa. Most members of the
Typhlopidae family (from the Greek typhlos, meaning blind) are small snakes
which feed on invertebrates and occur in tropical environments around the world. They
usually live underground or under other forms of cover and tend to lay only 5–12 eggs.
However, this species is a large family member which lays 50 eggs or more.*

Family Typhlopidae – Blind snakes (about 150 species). These are also small snakes which feed on invertebrates. They occur in tropical environments around the world, and tend to live underground or under other forms of cover. Although they also have a vestigial pelvic girdle and most appear to be oviparous, they differ from the Leptotyphlopidae and Anomalepidae in that they only have teeth along their upper jaw.

Family Anomalepidae – (about 20 species). Little is known about these small, burrowing snakes from tropical South America. They are similar in appearance to snakes from the two families mentioned above except they have teeth on both the upper and lower jaw and no vestigial pelvic girdle.

Family Uropeltidae – Shield-tailed and tube snakes (about 50 species). The tube snakes (sub-family Cylindrophinae), so called because of their body shape, are burrowing animals from southern Asia which grow up to 39 in (1 m) long, some of which feed on eels and other snakes. The shield-tailed snakes are in a different sub-family (Uropeltinae), but also have a burrowing lifestyle and feed on worms. They occur in Sri Lanka and southern India, some species growing up to 2 ft 5½ in (75 cm) in length. The end of their tails finishes with a single, large scale which may serve to protect the rear of the snakes as they burrow forward.

Family Aniliidae – The South American ringed snake (one species). The single member of this family has a striking, red and black banded pattern along its body, similar to the venomous coral snakes (from family Elapidae). It is mainly a burrowing animal, growing to around 2 ft 7½ in (80 cm) in length and feeding on a variety of prey including invertebrates, small reptiles and amphibians. Like many of the more primitive snakes, its head is narrow and it is unable to cope with bulky prey.

Family Xenopeltidae – The sunbeam or South Asian rainbow snake, *Xenopeltis unicolor*. The single species in this family, which grows up to 39 in (1 m) in length, is dark colored but iridescent, hence its two common names. It shows some advanced features such as having no limb or pelvic remains, a brille (see p. 20) covering the eye and large scales on its underside. However, it also has a small mouth like the more primitive snakes and only limited skull flexibility. It is mainly a burrowing species which feeds on other snakes and lizards.

Family Loxocemidae – Mexican dwarf python, *Loxocemus bicolor* (1 species). The single member of this family is anatomically similar to the sunbeam snake described above, although it has a vestigial pelvis. It lives in Central America but little is known of its ecology.

Family Boidae – Boas and pythons (about 75 species). The members of this family include the largest snakes in the world although some, such as the small, burrowing sand boas, only grow to about 39 in (1 m) in length. Their heads are well differentiated from their bodies and they differ from the more primitive families by having large mouths and flexible jaws. However, they also possess a vestigial pelvis and leg bones. Generally, pythons are oviparous and boas – which also tend to be less stocky – are ovoviviparous (the eggs are held in the mother's body until they hatch). They all use constriction to kill their prey and have a broad tropical and sub-tropical distribution.

Family Tropidophiidae – Forest boas (about 20 species). These relatively small and secretive snakes used to be included within the Boidae. They occur in the Caribbean region.

Family Bolyeridae – Round Island boas (two species). Round Island is near Mauritius and is the only place where these two endangered species occur. They used to be included within the Boidae but, like the Tropidophiidae, posses some more advanced anatomical features. They lack a vestigial pelvis and hind limbs.

Family Acrochordidae – File or wart snakes (three species). These are aquatic, ovoviviparous snakes which occur in coastal areas from south-east Asia to north Australia. They feed mainly on fish. Their name derives from their unusual, loose skin which is covered in small scales, giving them a grainy or warty appearance. They have the advanced features of a flexible skull and no vestigial pelvic remains.

Family Colubridae – Colubrid snakes (over 1650 species). Since this is by far the largest family, there is a great diversity in the appearance, physiology, behavior and

The amethyst python from Australia can grow up to 20 ft (6 m) in length.

ecology of the colubrids. However, they share the common features of having no vestigial pelvic remains, large scales along their underside, a brille (see p. 20) and, generally, a head well differentiated from the body and a large mouth. Some are venomous although they are usually not dangerous to humans since the venom fangs tend to be situated towards the back of the mouth. They have a wide distribution.

Family Elapidae – Elapid snakes (about 170 species). The elapids, which include the cobras, mambas, taipans and sea snakes, are believed to be closely related to the colubrids and are anatomically similar. They differ from colubrids in having tubular fangs set at the front of the mouth which, together with venom which can be potent, makes many species dangerous to humans. They occur in warm regions around the world apart from Europe. The largest species is the king cobra, or hamadryad, which can grow up to 16 ft 3 in (5 m) in length.

Family Atractaspididae – Mole vipers (about 15 species). These are burrowing snakes which are sometimes classified within the Colubridae or Elapidae. Although anatomically distinct from the Viperidae, they were originally classified as vipers since they have hinged fangs. Most live in southern and eastern Africa and feed on other burrowing reptiles.

Family Viperidae – Vipers (over 180 species). These snakes have the most sophisticated venom apparatus with hinged, tubular fangs set at the front of the mouth which can swing forward during a strike. They can be sub-divided into the true vipers and the pit vipers (which include the rattlesnakes). They occur on all continents except Antarctica (where no snakes occur) and Australia and at more extreme latitudes than other families. They tend to have shorter, thicker bodies than the elapids. Most species have elliptical pupils and some species are potentially dangerous.

General Snake Biology

Size, shape and skin – The elongate, 'serpentine' body shape is the most instantly recognizable feature of a snake, although this can vary from the long and thin form

The green mamba, an arboreal, venomous species which often hunts in the highest tops of trees.

of some arboreal species such as the green mamba to the short, massive forms of certain vipers. Body size also varies tremendously from only 6 in (15 cm) or so for some of the minute thread snakes up to a massive 30 ft (9 m) in length and 23½ stone (150 kg) in weight for the anaconda.

Many people are surprised to discover that the scaly skins of snakes are dry to the touch, unlike the moist, scale-less skins of frogs, newts and other amphibians. Scales serve to provide protection and help in locomotion; they are often used as a means of identifying species since they vary in size, number, texture and arrangement.

Snakes regularly shed their skins during a process called 'ecdysis'. The entire skin is removed in one smooth operation several times a year, the frequency of this depending on the species and the age of the animal, with younger snakes sloughing more often than older ones. The process begins with the skin coming away at the tip of the head, whereupon the snake rubs itself against objects, such as rocks and branches, so that the rest of the skin is turned inside-out and then peeled off like a sock being pulled off a foot.

Unlike lizards, snakes do not have movable eyelids. In the case of some of the more primitive burrowing snakes, such as the Typhlopidae, the eyes are small and covered by scales. In the more advanced snakes (e.g. families Xenopeltidae, Boidae, Elapidae and others) the eyes are covered by a 'brille' – a strong, transparent covering which provides protection. The brille also sloughs off with the rest of the skin during ecdysis.

A vast range in coloration is found amongst snakes. The function of coloration may be linked to camouflage or to provide a warning against potential aggressors (see p. 56). The colors we see are a result of special pigment cells in the dermis layer of the snake's skin, or of the refractive and reflective properties of the skin, or a combination of both. Dark, red and yellow colors tend to be due to the former and iridescent and green colors are due to the latter. The pigment melanin, which produces dark colors, can sometimes be so dominant that individuals of a species

The heat-sensitive 'pits' of this Wagler's pit viper are situated between its eyes and nostrils.

The emerald tree boa (top) is an arboreal species from South America. It has a prehensile tail to help anchor itself during strikes at birds, bats and arboreal mammals which it then kills by constriction. The Asian vine snake (bottom) also has adaptations for an arboreal lifestyle. It has keyhole-shaped pupils, and grooves running along its cheeks in front of the eyes, thus providing improved binocular vision to help it survive in a three-dimensional habitat.

can appear much darker than normal. For example, populations of adders on some islands off Scandinavia have a very high proportion of melanic individuals although the species is usually light colored with dark zigzag markings along the back. Conversely, an absence of melanin can result in albino individuals.

Internal anatomy – The skeleton of a snake basically consists of the skull, spine and ribs. The great majority of species have no limbs or limb girdles, although the more primitive snakes, as we have seen already, may have vestigial hind limbs and/or pelvic girdles. In male boas and pythons, for example, the vestigial limbs take the form of anal spurs or 'claws'. A large python has around 400 vertebrae and 300 ribs, providing great flexibility to its body, although the numbers of these bones vary depending on the species. The skulls of the more advanced snake families are flexible, with the upper and lower jaws only loosely connected to each other or to the cranium, giving them the ability to move apart and allow prey much larger than the size of their heads to be swallowed. The teeth of snakes vary considerably, with some of the more advanced species having the ability to inject venom into prey using fangs.

The internal organs of snakes tend to be elongated and displaced due to the serpentine body shape. A few species, such as some of the Boidae, have two functional lungs, but in most snakes the left lung is either absent or just a fraction of the size of the right lung. The digestive tract is quite short, as with many carnivorous animals.

Sensory abilities – Hearing in snakes is probably not well developed since they have no outer ear and only a very reduced middle ear. It seems likely that vibrations transmitted along the ground can be detected by a snake, although it is believed some arboreal species may be able to detect vibrations transmitted through the air. Sight is a much more important sense for snakes, apart from those which have a burrowing lifestyle. Generally, snake eyes can provide a wide field of vision since they are set on the side of the head. They have a certain degree of binocular vision, more so in certain arboreal species which provides them with an advantage when moving through tree canopies. Some species can detect color and, unlike other reptiles, many snakes also have the ability to focus images. Nocturnal species often have vertically slit pupils and diurnal species have round pupils, although exceptions include some vipers which hunt during the day but have vertical pupils.

In humans, the sense of smell allows us to detect chemicals in the air and we do this using olfactory receptors in our nose. Snakes can also smell and have nasal passages lined with receptors which play a similar role. However, snakes also have a 'vomeronasal' sense which is slightly different from the sense of smell. When you watch a snake, it is noticeable how often it flicks its forked tongue in the air or onto a surface. By doing this the tongue collects chemicals and then transfers them to the 'Jacobson's organ', a vomeronasal organ positioned inside the roof of its mouth which detects the chemicals present.

A few groups of snakes also have the added sensory ability to detect heat emitted by warm-blooded birds and mammals. The pit vipers have a deep dimple or 'pit' situated between the eye and nostril, lined with sensory cells able to detect infra-red heat. The pythons have a line of heat-sensitive pits along their upper lips. Some boas have a few heat-sensitive sensory cells within, rather than between, their scales.

Sound production – Perhaps the best-known examples of sound produced by snakes are the warning hisses, produced by inhaling and exhaling air, many species make when they are threatened. A few species, such as the king cobra, can produce very low-frequency hisses and this is thought to be an effect produced by pockets along their windpipes which act as resonating chambers. Such 'growls' may be picked up by other individuals of the same species. The tail rattles of rattlesnakes, which are made from loosely interlocking, horny segments, can be shaken to warn or confuse predators whereas the saw-scaled or carpet viper has keel-shaped scales which can be rubbed together to produce a rasping sound when it feels threatened.

A rattlesnake in a high state of alert, body drawn up and tongue picking up chemical signals.

An American sidewinder rattlesnake showing the classic sidewinding
style of locomotion in the Anza-Borrego Desert of California. Many
other species will also adopt this technique on loose, sandy surfaces.

Locomotion – Despite the fact that snakes lack legs, they are still able to move effectively through different media such as water and forest canopies and on sand. 'Straight' or 'linear locomotion' is often used by some of the larger species such as boas and pythons. This is where a snake lifts and moves forward small groups of scales in a continuous series of waves, then re-anchors them and uses the scales to provide grip to pull its body forward with its muscles. In this way the snake appears to glide forward without any sideways body flexing.

'Lateral undulation' is the more recognizable serpentine-style of locomotion during which all regions of the snake's body are moving relative to the surrounding medium. The fastest snakes use this method, including the East African black mamba which has been measured traveling at 7 mph (11 kmph). There are other variations on these methods, the best known being the 'sidewinding' style used by the American sidewinder rattlesnake and other desert species, although many species will use it when moving across loose, sandy material. This graceful method involves the head and a loop of the body being thrown ahead and to the side in a series of continuous movements.

Heat and temperature control – It is a surprise for many people to learn that snakes can sometimes be warm to the touch. Snakes, like other reptiles, are 'ectothermic', that is they obtain their body heat mostly from external sources such as the direct solar radiation of the sun or through being in contact with warm objects. This is sometimes described as being 'cold-blooded' but is an inaccurate description of snake body temperature since, under certain conditions, it may be relatively high. For example, in the constantly warm conditions of a tropical forest where the ambient temperature is high, the body temperature of a resident snake will also be high. In the more extreme conditions encountered at higher altitudes or higher latitudes, ambient temperatures may be quite low, so snakes often need to bask in the warming rays of the sun to raise their body temperature.

The ability to select optimal body temperatures is important for snakes as it affects so many aspects of their physiology and performance. Food digestion, egg production, speed of locomotion, striking speeds and many other factors are all dependent on the body temperature of the snake. Therefore they may thermoregulate using a variety of behavioral techniques such as selecting suitable places to bask and timing their basking periods in order to make use of available solar radiation. Some can even change the shape of their bodies: the adder, for example, can flatten itself into a ribbon to present more surface area and catch more of the sun's rays. In this way, some species can maintain their body temperature very precisely at high levels during the day even though they may be living in a cool climate. During cold times of the day or year, there is much less opportunity to get heat in these ways so snakes become inactive and retreat below ground, sometimes for months on end.

Reproduction – Most snakes are solitary animals although some species which live in cooler climates will overwinter together in communal shelters. Otherwise, the mating period tends to be the only time when individuals make much contact with each other. At such times the males of some species, such as certain elapids and vipers, engage in ritualistic combat where males rise up in front of each other, sometimes with the hind parts of their bodies coiled together, and try to bump and push each other to the ground. Some male colubrids have more aggressive battles and will try to bite each other.

Mating begins once males have detected the characteristic chemical odors, or 'pheromones', produced by receptive females. The male moves along the female's back, until eventually the couple wind their tails around each other and press genital openings together. The male has two 'hemipenes' which are normally sheathed inside his body but during copulation they become erect and he will try to insert one into the female's genital opening. Coupling usually lasts an hour or two but can take a lot longer. In some species, such as the garter snake of North America, a female can attract numerous males when she is receptive, resulting in a mating ball orgy.

Adders raising their body temperatures by basking in the sun.

Females may not always be fertilized immediately. Some biologists believe that female adders can, under certain conditions, store sperm for at least one year before using it to fertilize their eggs. This controversial suggestion is still up for debate, as is the view that a single female can store the sperm of several different males after different matings. The sperm from several matings can fertilize a single batch of eggs, the result being a litter of young adders with different fathers.

Most snakes are oviparous which means they lay eggs, which have to be laid in sites which provide the right amount of warmth and humidity for incubation; this is particularly important for those species living in cooler environments, such as the grass snake in the northern European part of its range, which lays its eggs in rotting vegetation such as farm manure heaps and garden compost heaps.

In ovoviviparous snakes, on the other hand, the eggs are held inside the mother until they are ready or almost ready to hatch. The mother is less mobile during this period and therefore more vulnerable to predators, less able to catch prey and has to spend more time thermoregulating to ensure the eggs develop quickly inside her. However, it does mean that the young are given a head start and do not have to spend time developing in vulnerable eggs in an incubation site outside the mother's body. In cooler environments ovoviviparous species are more common since there tend to be few sites sufficiently warm to incubate eggs.

After laying eggs or giving birth to developed young, adult snakes have little or no part in parental care. There are exceptions, such as the female king cobra which builds a two-story nest underground with a basement for its eggs and the upper floor for either the male or female adult which defends the nest. Some female pythons, such as the Indian python will lay eggs and then coil themselves around them. They can raise the temperature of the eggs above ambient levels by a few degrees through spasmodically contracting their muscles in a process which is similar to shivering.

Feeding is another interesting aspect of snake natural history which will be considered in detail later on.

*Pueblan milk snake (a false coral snake) with eggs. About
70 per cent of all snake species lay eggs, the remainder giving birth
to live young after the eggs hatch within the females' bodies.*

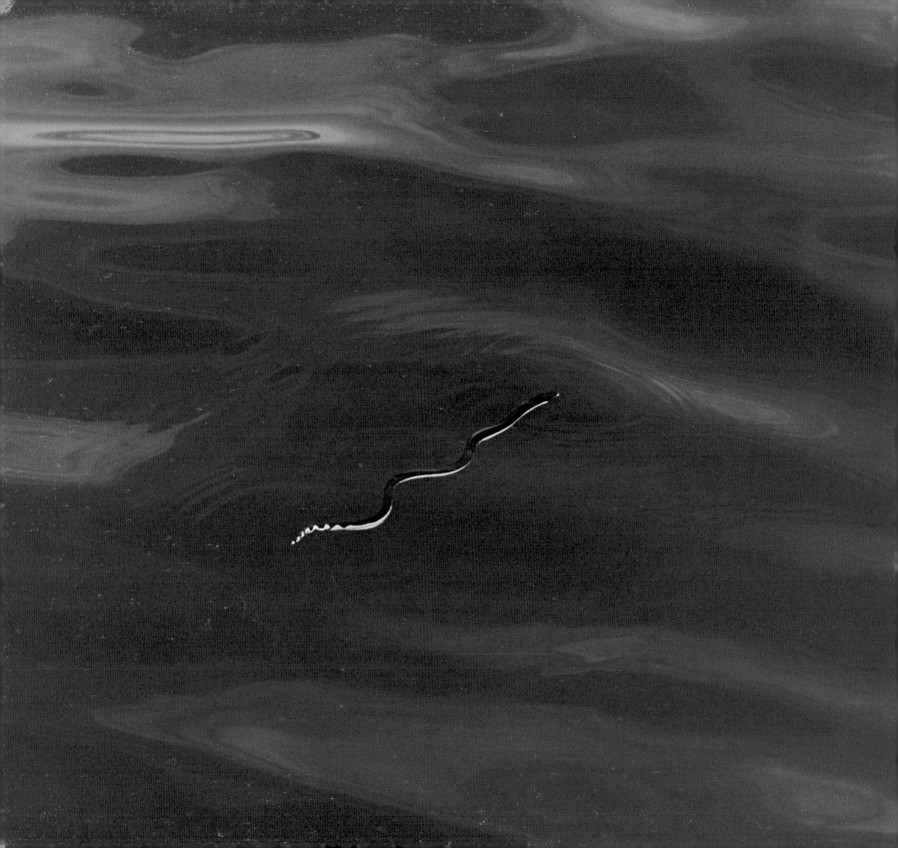

The Diversity of Snakes

So far we have looked at some of the common threads in snake biology. However, with so many species of snake in the world distributed throughout a wide variety of environments, the diversity of snake natural history is enormous and it is important that we take some time to examine some of this in more detail, although it will only be possible to have a cursory glance at this subject. Despite the fact that snakes are not as well studied as some other vertebrate groups, there is a large amount of research that we can draw upon to give us some insight into snake ecology. What follows is a description of some of the characteristics of snakes found in a range of broad environmental types.

Marine

Some scientists are now coming to the view that snakes originated in the seas. However, although the descendants of these marine ancestors eventually moved onto land, a few snake groups have returned to the sea. The three members of the family Acrochordidae, the wart snakes, are all aquatic and one species, *Acrochordus granulatus*, lives in both marine and freshwater habitats. There are also certain colubrid snakes that inhabit marine, estuarine or salt marsh habitats. However, the best-known marine species are the sea snakes, a group of elapids belonging to their own sub-family (Hydrophinae) and consisting of the sea kraits and the 'true' sea snakes.

There are about fifty species of sea snakes which occur throughout the Pacific and Indian Oceans as far north as the Persian Gulf. None have reached the Atlantic Ocean. The sea kraits are more primitive and have features more in common with terrestrial snake species, such as broad overlapping scales on their underside, which some sea kraits (those of the genus *Laticauda*) use to help crawl themselves onto land in order to rest between feeding bouts and lay eggs in deep crevices. When the young hatch

A brightly colored yellow-bellied sea snake, perhaps the world's most abundant reptile.

from the eggs, they crawl directly into the sea to begin their marine existence. The females of true sea snakes, on the other hand, are ovoviviparous and give birth to live young at sea which means they never need to come ashore. True sea snakes, therefore, do not have the well-developed underside scales of sea kraits.

The tip of a sea snake's tail is flattened to help propel it through the water when swimming. Internally, they have a very large lung running from head to tail. This is believed to aid both buoyancy and oxygen needs, although they have the ability to provide for 30 per cent of their oxygen requirements by respiring through their skin. Some species can dive to depths of 160 ft (50 m) and remain submerged for over two hours. Since they live in a highly saline environment, they have a special gland under their tongue to expel salt from the body. Other marine reptiles, such as turtles and iguanas, have similar glands.

Many species of sea snake catch fish by probing the nooks and crannies of rocks and, upon finding their prey, loop their bodies to block the exits before biting and subduing them. However, three species of true sea snake (*Emydocephalus annulatus*, *E. ijimae* and *Aipysurus eydouxi*) feed exclusively on fish eggs. Interestingly, these three species possess a special muscle on the floor of their mouth called a 'geniomucosalis'. This structure has also been found in some of the more primitive snake families and can create a suction effect, allowing them to suck up ants, termites and other small soil animals. Since the stomachs of the three sea snakes that eat fish eggs have been found to contain large quantities of sand it is probable that the eggs are gathered off the sea floor using a sort of vacuum-cleaner effect.

The yellow-bellied sea snake is also a true sea snake but since it feeds in surface waters, and is therefore not restricted to the shallow coastal waters like sea snakes, which feed on the sea floor, it has a wide oceanic occurrence. Its hunting strategy is simply to lie on the surface of the water and, when a fish comes to shelter underneath, to strike. This species is a relatively weak swimmer and drifts with the oceanic currents. Individuals may die when they drift into cold waters or are washed up on shore, where they are more or less helpless. It cleans itself by forming a knot of its body and rubbing

*Yellow-lipped sea krait on Snake Island, Sabah, Malaysia. This species of
sea snake often comes ashore to thermoregulate and to lay eggs in damp sand.*

off encrusting organisms, a process which is aided every 14 days when it sheds its skin, although older animals are occasionally found with encrusting barnacles on their tails. It has been suggested that this species could be the world's most numerous reptile since it is sometimes recorded in colossal shoals.

The venom of sea snakes is extremely toxic but the animals are very placid by nature and, on the occasions when they do bite humans in self-defence, venom is not always released from the fangs. The yellow-bellied sea snake does not appear to have many predators which may be due to its brilliant black and yellow warning coloration. Other sea snakes also have bold colors and patterning. Less conspicuous species may be taken by sea eagles and sharks, with mortality among young individuals being particularly high.

Freshwater

Although most snakes are quite capable of swimming and moving through watery environments, some have specialized to live in freshwater habitats such as rivers, lakes, ponds and marshes. Most freshwater species are colubrids, although there are also members of the Boidae, Elapidae and Viperidae which live semi-aquatic lives, in addition to the fully aquatic members of the Acrochordidae mentioned above.

Among the colubrid snakes, the sub-families Natricinae and Homalopsinae, in particular, have many members adapted to aquatic lifestyles. The Natricinae include species familiar to many Europeans such as the viperine snake, found throughout south-west Europe, which has a semi-aquatic lifestyle, and the grass snake, which has a wider distribution and will often forage in wetlands. Nearly all 35 or so species in the Homalopsinae are aquatic and have compressed tails (like the sea snakes), give birth to live young and have eyes and nostrils on top of their heads. One member is the tentacled snake, a fully aquatic freshwater species from the Indochinese region which grows up to 35½ in (90 cm) long and is so called because of the two

After hunting in cool water, the viperine snake basks in the sun to warm up again.

tentacle-like structures which project forwards from its mouth, the function of which is unknown. It is the only known snake species to include plants in its diet. It has also lost the broad underside scales common to other terrestrial colubrid species which means, like the true sea snakes, it is completely helpless on dry land.

One of the most impressive and best-known freshwater snakes is the anaconda, of the family Boidae. The anaconda occurs throughout the northern region of South America where it feeds on a variety of prey including caimans, turtles and mammals, killing its prey by constriction. It can live in rivers and marshes but is also capable of climbing trees.

Fiction, rather than fact, has given the anaconda an unfair reputation.

Although the anaconda is undoubtedly an impressive and giant snake, it has developed an unjustified notoriety and there are many stories of early explorers recording enormous specimens, usually with little evidence to back up their claims. For example, an officer in the Royal Artillery who was leading a survey of a remote area of the Amazon Basin in 1907, recorded how he watched a large anaconda surface near the dugout canoes of his survey team before crawling onto the bank to escape. He claimed that he shot the snake and measured it at 62 ft 4 in (19 m) long. Interestingly, the specimen was not collected! Even harder to believe is the 1948 Brazilian news story of a 154 ft (47 m) animal which was killed only after battling with a detachment of soldiers and demolishing a few buildings. Similar stories have been repeated over the years but the generally accepted and reliable maximum is around 30 ft (9 m) in length and 23½ stone (150 kg) in weight. Animals greater than 19 ft 8 in (6 m) in length are very rare. Even so, the anaconda is the heaviest snake species although other members of the family Boidae, such as the Rock or African python can also reach around 30 ft (9 m) and the more slender reticulated python may grow slightly longer at 33 ft (10 m).

Recently studies have been made on the reproductive ecology of the anaconda in Venezuelan wetlands. For just a few weeks during the breeding season of mid February to mid May, some females become attractive to males, with the result that anything from one to twelve males will coil around single females, forming impressive 'breeding balls' which stay together from two to four weeks. Females are typically three to five times larger than their mates and heavier females tend to attract longer, and a greater number of, males. Since it is therefore likely that several males have the opportunity to mate with a single female during this period, it may be that the sperm of the various males have to compete to fertilize her eggs. For the entire six- to eight-month period of gestation which follows fertilization, the females do not eat, possibly to avoid the risk of damaging the developing young when attempting to capture prey. Large females can give birth to around seventy live young, each weighing 8–9½ oz (250–300 g).

Arid and Semi-arid Environments

In contrast to the aquatic snakes, other species survive in habitats where water can be in short supply. Whereas amphibians have a moist skin and need to return to water to breed, snakes and other reptiles have fewer restrictions which has meant they have become successful colonisers of many of the world's arid and semi-arid regions.

Snakes lose only small amounts of water in their feces which helps to reduce water loss under desert conditions. Since they are carnivorous, their prey are also rich in water content. Nevertheless, they need to avoid high environmental temperatures and do so by burrowing or seeking out cool rock crevices and holes in the heat of the day and restricting activity to the cooler periods. The Asian sand viper is an example of a snake which burrows to avoid the sun. It can lie on the surface of the sand and then sweep its body from side to side, gradually sinking down until only its eyes and nostrils are visible. This leaves the animal hidden and in an ideal situation to ambush passing prey.

A number of snake families are represented in these types of environments, such as the sand boa of India from the family Boidae, the Californian king snake of family Colubridae and the death adder of Australia from the Elapidae. The family Viperidae is very well represented in deserts, both the true vipers such as the saw-scaled viper from the Asian and African deserts, and the pit vipers such as the diamondback rattlesnake from North America.

Moving over very loose sand can also be a problem and snakes will often use the 'sidewinding' movement, mentioned before, to negotiate such surfaces. Distantly related viper species such as the sidewinder rattlesnake of the North American deserts and the horned viper of the Great Palearctic Desert, both commonly use the sidewinding form of movement in their natural habitat.

Forest

Snakes can be found living in many types of forests, although the number of species is greatest in the tropical rain forests. Some snakes live on forest floors, others spend much of their entire lives off the ground and in the trees, others can utilize both layers.

Many tree-living, or 'arboreal', snakes tend to have common characteristics which help them deal with their high-rise existence. For example, these features are exhibited by members of four distantly related genera in the Colubridae, namely *Thelotornis* from Africa, *Ahaetulla* in Asia and *Oxybelis* and *Uromacer* from the Neotropical Region. Despite being distantly related, all four genera have evolved slender body shape, camouflage coloration, large eyes and a greater degree of binocular vision. This is an example of 'convergence' which means that, over time, evolution has produced increasing similarity in certain characteristics in groups of organisms which were initially different.

The Australian desert is home to the woma python. This one is near Uluru (Ayers Rock).

The paradise tree snake of Asia has evolved the ultimate form of swift movement amongst the tree canopy. This slender animal can launch itself from branches and glide to other trees. It does this by contracting the underside of its body into a concave surface and using it to provide a type of parachute effect.

The improved binocular vision capability of arboreal snakes results from their narrow heads and snouts which allows the visual fields of the two eyes to overlap at the front. Some snakes, such as the East Indian long-nosed tree snake also have grooves in front of the eyes and along the cheeks. Binocular vision presumably gives arboreal species the ability to judge distances better, particularly valuable when moving between branches in the tree canopy.

Arboreal snakes may also have angled scales on their underside which help them grip surfaces when climbing, and some have a prehensile tail which can be used to grip a branch while the rest of the body stretches forward to move onto another branch. This is a feature of Wagler's pit viper even though most other vipers, which are predominantly ground-living, have no such ability.

A species of twig snake, *Thelotornis capensis*, of southern Africa has the characteristic slender body shape of arboreal species. However, it tends to lie in wait for prey on the very lowest branches with the upshot that it can feed both on animals living in the tree, such as chameleons and tree frogs, as well as on ground-living species such as certain lizards and burrowing toads. Twig snakes are sometimes called 'bird snakes' since it was believed that, being arboreal, birds formed a major part of their diet. However, more detailed study has shown

Blunthead tree snake, French Guiana.

that although they will take birds when possible, it does not appear to happen very often and this is probably also true for many other arboreal species. In fact, the example of *T. capensis* suggests it may have adapted features suitable for the tree-living lifestyle not so much for feeding on arboreal prey but for protection from predators. This could also be the case for other arboreal snakes.

Some snakes have even been forced into a life in the tree canopy. A tiny species of thread snake, *Leptotyphlops dulcis* of family Leptotyphlopidae, which normally has a burrowing lifestyle, also has the ability to climb trees. However, scientists studying eastern screech owls in Texas discovered another way that the snakes traveled to the tree tops when the birds were observed carrying live ones back to their nests. Screech owls normally kill their prey before returning home so this appeared to be unusual behavior. On closer examination, anything from one to fifteen live snakes were found burrowing into the debris lining the bottom of the nests. Further investigation showed that owl nestlings which shared a nest with live-in thread snakes suffered lower mortality and grew faster than those which did not. The reason for this may be that the snakes feed on the larvae of flies which parasitize the owl nestlings and also on other fly larvae which feed on the cached food held in the nest for the developing birds. In this way, the owls benefit from having live thread snakes in their nests, although it is not known if the snakes benefit from the arrangement.

Some species live on the forest floor and one of the most spectacular examples is the largest of all true vipers, the Gaboon viper of the central African forests. This animal grows up to 19 lb 11 oz (9 kg) in weight and 5 ft 11 in (1.8 m) in length. It lies in wait on the forest floor, hidden amongst the leaves by its camouflage-pattern skin, and ambushes prey when they are within striking distance. The venom is injected with the help of two formidable 2 in (5 cm) fangs, the largest of any snake. Since it is restricted to a forest-floor lifestyle, it has a much bulkier and broader body shape than arboreal species. In the South American forests, the fer-de-lance is another well-known, large, venomous viper which inhabits the forest floor. The fer-de-lance is a pit viper that can grow up to 5 ft 11 in (1.8 m) long and is responsible for the deaths of several hundred people every year. It is incredibly productive and, in exceptional cases, has been known to give birth to around one hundred young.

The green camouflage and prehensile tail of the green tree python from Australasia are adaptations to a tree-living lifestyle.

Hunters and the Hunted

Hunting Strategies and Finding Prey

Snakes use two main strategies to catch their prey. The first is the 'sit and wait' technique where the animal simply waits in a certain location and then ambushes prey which happen to pass within reach. The advantages of this method are that it requires little energy and the snake is less likely to be spotted by potential predators, but the risk is that there may be long periods of time spent waiting for food to pass within reach. The other technique is 'foraging' in which the snake actively searches for prey.

Different snakes rely on different sets of senses during different stages of catching prey. In rattlesnakes, for example, a combination of sensory information from the eyes, heat-sensitive pits on the head, the Jacobson's organ and nasal passages are used and these affect the snake's behavior before, during and after a prey animal is struck, although auditory stimuli play little role. Visual and thermal cues are most important to rattlesnakes before the strike, and chemical cues are more important after the strike when the prey animal is released from the jaws and has to be followed until it succumbs to the venom.

Catching and Subduing Prey

Snakes can catch prey in a number of ways. Those which feed on small prey such as invertebrates can simply grab them with their mouths and then swallow them. Larger prey need to be subdued first and constriction is one method commonly used by some colubrids and the pythons and boas. The purpose of constriction is not to crush the prey to death, but to suffocate it by grabbing the prey by the mouth, wrapping one or more body coils around it and then squeezing in order to prevent it ventilating. Once the animal is dead, it is swallowed. The largest animal recorded that was killed and swallowed by any snake was a 130 lb (59 kg) impala,

Boelen's python from the highlands of Papua New Guinea.

taken by a rock python. Some species, such as the smooth snake which occurs across much of Europe, uses a constriction technique but will start to swallow the animal before it is suffocated.

Snakes are well known for their use of venom in attack and defense. In some ways, all snakes can be considered venomous in that they all produce a range of enzymes in their mouth which initiate the process of digestion before the prey is swallowed. However, we tend to think a snake is truly venomous when it has

The boomslang can enlarge its neck with air to look bigger.

specialized teeth which enable it to deliver the venom into the prey by injection. Only three snake families, the colubrids, elapids and vipers, have members that are venomous.

Most venomous colubrids are not regarded as being particularly dangerous to humans because they have fangs at the back of their mouth, which makes it difficult for them to inflict a harmful bite. Such 'back-fanged' snakes have several grooved teeth which are larger than the others. When a prey animal is caught, it is manipulated to the back of the mouth where the snake chews on it, thus breaking the skin and allowing the venom to enter the victim's bloodstream. Only the larger venomous colubrids, such as the boomslang, an arboreal species from the forests of Africa known to have caused human deaths, pose serious threats to people. The boomslang has a potent venom and fangs closer to the front of the mouth than other colubrids.

The fangs of this eyelash palm pit viper normally rest in the two fleshy sheaths in the top of the mouth.

The elapids include a number of well-known poisonous and dangerous snakes such as the cobras, mambas, sea snakes and taipans. They have tubular fangs at the front of the mouth and when prey are struck, they are usually held in the jaws until the venom takes effect before being swallowed.

The vipers have the most sophisticated venom apparatus, consisting of hinged, tubular fangs at the front of the mouth. The fangs normally rest in the roof of the mouth in fleshy sheaths but, during a striking action, the mouth opens and the fangs swing down and point forward so that they can be plunged full force into the flesh of a prey or aggressor and the venom injected. The viper then withdraws its fangs and allows the victim to move away. The snake will follow the prey while the venom is taking effect and, once it is subdued, will collect and swallow it. It has recently been found that certain rattlesnakes can control the amount of venom they deliver during a strike and will inject larger amounts into larger-sized prey to ensure speedy deaths.

Venom

Snake venom is an amazing cocktail of chemicals, the composition of which not only varies between species but can also change in individual snakes as they grow older. Also, in some species the venom of one fang may be different in appearance and composition to that of the other fang.

It was Napoleon Bonaparte's brother, Lucien, who discovered that snake venom is protein in nature. The complexity and variety of the proteins that make up snake venom is a reason why they produce such a range of effects on their victims. First of all there are the toxins, including the so-called 'neurotoxins', which can affect the nervous system and cause paralysis. There are also, among others, 'hemorragines', which can affect the walls of blood vessels causing hemorrhaging, 'cardiotoxins' and 'sarafotoxins', which can induce cardiac arrest, and 'myotoxins', which cause muscular degeneration. Despite the commonly stated generality that elapid venom tends to affect the nervous system and viper venom tends to act

Mozambique spitting cobra. The venom is projected at the
eyes of potential predators by rapidly squeezing it out of the fangs by muscular
action, then blowing it by a sharp expulsion of air from the lungs. Spitting cobras are often
very aggressive and if the venom enters a person's eyes it can cause severe pain
and has to be washed out quickly before permanent damage is caused.

Wagler's pit viper, an arboreal species from south-east Asia.
Although many arboreal snakes are slender, day-hunting animals with narrow,
elongated heads, this slow-moving species is nocturnal and stocky with
a massive head. It has a prehensile tail to help grasp vegetation.

on the blood, this does not always hold true.

Enzymes are types of proteins that also occur in snake venom and can produce a toxic effect. However their main function is to speed the digestive process so that when a snake bites its prey, digestion can start even before it is swallowed. There are also other proteins present in venom which have a variety of functions such as disrupting the blood-clotting process and increasing bleeding or, at the other extreme, stimulating blood clotting.

Despite the powerful effects of such venom, some species such as the Californian ground squirrel have managed to develop immunity. Ground squirrels which live in areas where the predatory northern Pacific rattlesnake occurs, have been found to be three to five times more effective in neutralizing rattlesnake venom than those from rattlesnake-free areas, and the immunity is greater the denser the local rattlesnake population. This is an example of selective resistance to venom evolving in ground squirrel populations depending on how likely they are to encounter rattlesnakes. Ground squirrels have also developed defensive behaviors such as leaping and throwing stones at rattlesnakes, and can weigh up the risks of defending their young from a rattler in a dark burrow by listening to the sound of the rattles – deeper rattles imply larger snakes from which the squirrels are more likely to retreat.

Specialists

Although all snakes are predatory and feed exclusively on animals (apart from the tentacled snake which may also feed on vegetation), their diets vary greatly, with some having particular specializations. Certain sea snakes, for example, are specialist fish-egg feeders. The fifteen or so *Aparallactus* species feed mainly on centipedes, whereas the colubrid sub-families Pareinae and Dipsadinae feed on mollusks. The Dipsadinae are arboreal and have a hook-shaped lower jaw which helps them extract snails from their shells, whereas the Pareinae prey on slugs. Only one snake, the North American water moccasin, or 'cottonmouth', is known to feed on carrion although it usually takes live amphibians and fish.

Quite a number of species are 'ophiophagous', which means they feed on other snake species. The North American king snake will take rattlesnakes and the king cobra of south-east Asia, is also a snake-eating specialist.

Probably some of the best-known specialists are the egg-eating ('oophagous') colubrid snakes belonging to the genera *Dasypeltis* of the Saharan savannah and *Elachistodon* of India. They have the ability to open their jaws and engulf eggs far larger than their normal body diameter. Eggs are ingested whole and then swallowed as far as the neck; the neck vertebrae have spiny projections, which pierce the egg wall. The egg is then crushed, the contents swallowed, and the egg shell regurgitated.

Many species, such as this bright-ringed snake, eat other snakes.

Defense Strategies

Although snakes are predatory in nature, they also form part of the diet of many other predators. They may become the prey of other snake species, or of other reptiles such as alligators, crocodiles or large monitor lizards. Birds of prey, such as eagles and falcons, will feed on snakes including venomous species like cobras. One bird of prey in particular, the tall and long-legged secretary bird of eastern and southern Africa, is well known as a predator of snakes although it will also feed on a variety of other small animals. Various Galliformes (pheasants, fowl, turkeys and related birds) and some crows take snakes. Amongst the mammals, the most famous snake predators are the mongooses, with a reputation bolstered by *The Jungle Book*, Rudyard Kipling's tale of the battles between Rikki-tikki-tavi and the cobras Nag and Nagaina. Although mongooses will take snakes, most species are opportunistic and feed on small

This species of egg-eating snake, Dasypeltis scabra, pictured swallowing a
bird's egg, is the most common of the six African egg-eating snakes in the Dasypeltis
genus. When threatened, this non-venomous snake can rub its scales together to create
a startling, rasping noise. The effect may be enhanced by the fact that a similar display
is used by the venomous saw-scaled viper which lives in the same area.

vertebrates, invertebrates and even fruit. Hedgehogs are known to feed on various snake species, although they too are opportunists. Wild pigs, jackals, various members of the cat family, genets and even false vampire bats all occasionally take snakes.

Many snake predators tackle venomous species even though they risk death or injury. Predators may rely on their agility to avoid being bitten before inflicting a lethal bite on their prey. Other species depend on some sort of protective covering, such as the feathers of birds or spines of a hedgehog. Hedgehogs, together with some other predators, also have a degree of immunity to snake venom. Scientists have isolated three proteins from hedgehog blood serum which act against the proteins of adder venom and prevent hemorrhaging, a serious effect of adder bite in normal circumstances.

In order to avoid or combat attacks from predators and other aggressors, snakes have evolved a variety of ways to defend themselves. Some species have body markings which make them very hard to see in their natural habitat and which help them hide from predators as well as from potential prey. Certain arboreal species such as the twig snakes have taken this a stage further, since they not only have coloration which blends in with the tree vegetation they inhabit, they also have long, thin bodies which can appear quite twig-like.

In contrast, other species have very bright coloration which functions as an advertisement to potential predators that they are dangerous. Many other animals, such as wasps, ladybirds, poison arrow frogs and skunks, also use bright and bold colors to advertise that they are harmful in some way. Some of the best-known examples are the fifty or so species of coral snakes, elapids belonging to the genera *Micrurus* and *Micruroides*, which range from the Southern U.S. to Argentina and have a fairly powerful venom which can have a strong effect on humans. Coral snakes have characteristic ring markings of red, white or yellow and black. Interestingly, there are

The variable coral snake is a 'true' coral snake and is brightly colored as a warning to potential predators that it is venomous.

other species of snakes which live in the same region and have similar coloration and therefore appear to mimic the coral snakes, including the so-called false coral snakes of the genus *Erythrolampus* which are only mildly poisonous, and the harmless milk snakes of the genus *Lampropeltis*. Biologists working in Costa Rica have tested the effectiveness of these warning colors by leaving plasticine snake models in forests and then later retrieving them to count the number of peck marks left on them by birds. Some of the models had typical coral-snake markings whereas other models were colored brown. The results were that brown models had many more peck marks than the red, black and yellow models, suggesting that birds avoided the bright coloration.

Bright colors are also used by a few colubrids such as the North American ringnecks. Although they have a camouflage coloration on their dorsal sides, when threatened they show the brightly colored yellow or red underside of their bodies, presumably sufficient to startle some aggressors.

Other lines of defense may not be so passive. Many snakes will immediately flee to safety when confronted with danger, although some may wait until the last moment in case their camouflage coloration works. Snakes will often stay close to the safety of shelter such as dense vegetation.

If fleeing is not possible, snakes will use various displays to intimidate or confuse potential predators, or warn larger animals of their presence before they are accidentally trampled. Hissing is a well-known example that many species, not only venomous ones, may use and it can be very effective, as anyone who has confronted an angry, noisy snake will testify. Rattlesnakes also warn aggressors by using sound, in their case by rattling their tail. The impact of hissing may be reinforced by other displays, most famously by the raised hoods of cobras which makes them appear larger. Other species, such as the boomslang try to create a similar effect by blowing themselves up with air, which can expand the size of its neck in this way when threatened. Another form of warning display is used by the North American water moccasin which is also called the cottonmouth since when threatened it will open its mouth wide, revealing a startling white interior which contrasts with its dark body color.

Such warning displays are often combined with a posture designed for quick, defensive strikes. Snakes may coil up their body with the head and front part of the body raised above in an S-shape, the head pointing towards the source of danger. If such displays fail, then venomous snakes will strike and try to inject venom. Non-venomous snakes will also strike at an adversary even though they can do no harm, but potential predators may still back off. Although they can bite, the so-called spitting cobras of Africa and parts of Asia, such as the Mozambique spitting cobra, and other cobras of the *Naja* genus, can also project venom several yards at the eyes of potential predators.

A series of different defensive techniques may be used. For example, the grass snake is a fast species that will try to flee from danger in the first instance but, if caught, will hiss and even occasionally bite if provoked, although it is harmless to humans and has only short teeth. It can also expel a foul-smelling secretion from glands in the anal region which can most readily be compared with the smell of rotten garlic. Our own experience of working with

Defensive display of an Arabian cobra.

this species is that this unpleasant display can also be combined with a regurgitation of stomach contents, enough to put off many aggressors and even well-meaning researchers. If all this fails, some individuals will feign death by flipping over onto their backs and remaining motionless with their mouths open and tongues hanging out.

Snakes and People

Beliefs

Snakes are members of that unfortunate animal club, which includes the bats, wolves and sharks, which has a major image problem. Their bad image has been moulded and reinforced by myths and folklore which still persist as we move into the twenty-first century. In 1856 the naturalist Oliver Goldsmith wrote, in what was claimed to be a scientific account of natural history at the time, 'the serpent has, from the beginning, been the enemy of man: and it has hitherto continued to terrify and annoy him, notwithstanding all the arts that have been practised to destroy it'. This sort of attitude, which sometimes verges on the hysterical, has not helped the snakes' cause.

Snakes have often been portrayed in religion as symbols of evil, for example in *The Book of Genesis* of the Christian and Jewish traditions, which describes how the serpent was involved in the temptation and fall of man and was punished by God: 'Upon thy belly shalt thou go, and dust thou shalt eat all the days of thy life'. In Hindu religion, the god Vritra is a harmful giant snake which holds the earth's waters and provokes droughts, but who battles Indra, the god of warriors and the rains. When Indra defeats Vritra and slices opens his stomach, the waters escape and the rain falls.

In some cultures snakes can also be symbols of good. The rainbow serpent is common to many Australian aboriginal dreamtime stories, and is often portrayed as a giant snake associated with creation and the provision of water. Common cobras have two spots on their necks and an Indian story describes how this is believed to be a mark of divine gratitude from Buddha, who awoke from sleeping in the sun to find himself being shaded by a cobra with its open hood. In many cultures the snake is associated with medicine and healing. The symbol of Asclepius, son of Apollo, who was the ancient Greek god of medicine, was a staff with a serpent coiled around it and similar symbols have been adopted by the modern medical profession.

Bredl's carpet python in the MacDonnell Range, central Australia.

Snakes – Costs and Benefits

What are the facts when it comes to the interaction of people with snakes? Do we really have much to fear from them? It is true that there are parts of the world where venomous snakes can pose a danger to local people. This is particularly the case where populations of venomous species coincide with human populations of peasant farmers who work bare-footed and lightly clothed, where people are more remote from modern medical facilities and where increased numbers of snake prey, such as rodents, occur as a result of poor hygiene. For example, in India, about 12,000 people die each year from snake bites and there are 200 hospital cases per 100,000 inhabitants. This compares to 5 hospital cases per 100,000 inhabitants in the U.S.A., and very few deaths. Few hospital incidences and deaths occur in Europe and even in Australia, which has a high abundance of venomous species. Unfortunately, some of the hospital cases that do occur in the latter countries often result from a dangerous cocktail of macho exhibitionism and alcohol.

However, we also need to appreciate the beneficial role of snakes. Because snakes are both predators and preyed upon, they form important components of natural food webs and their loss would have repercussions on other species living in their ecological communities. There may be more direct, material benefits that people gain from snakes, such as providing a source of food in some tribal cultures. Snakes are also eaten as a delicacy, and used as a source of traditional medicines and snake skin in some countries, although such large-scale exploitation can be harmful to snake populations. Components of snake venom have been isolated and used for a variety of modern medical purposes relating to, amongst other things, the function of blood coagulation and the treatment of high blood pressure. But there are also the less tangible benefits that snakes provide as part of our cultural and natural heritage. They play an important role in our religions, cultures, stories and entertainment, and provide a source of enjoyment, or at least fascination, to people who watch them in the wild, at zoos, on television or who even keep them as pets.

Snakes play a special role in the myths and religions of many cultures around the world. Although Western cultures usually portray the snake as a symbol of evil, the same is not always true elsewhere. In some parts of India, for example, the highly venomous common cobra is treated with reverence and respect.

The Conservation of Snakes

Too many wildlife books include sad tales of loss and destruction and unfortunately this one is no different. Snakes have generally suffered at the hands of humans, to the extent that some species are now seriously under threat.

Habitat loss – Habitat destruction is probably the major cause of decline for several species. Many people will immediately think of the large-scale loss of the world's tropical forests in this context, and this is certainly having major impacts. However it is also happening on the doorsteps of the richer countries of the western world. In Britain, for example, some of the best habitat for reptiles, including the three native snake species (the smooth snake, the adder and the grass snake, which all have some level of legal protection), are the lowland heaths of southern England. The author Thomas Hardy set many of his stories around these great Wessex heathlands but in his time they used to stretch continuously for miles and miles. Now only small pockets remain, fragmented and often poorly managed, yet even these precious small remnants are still being lost to development, woodland encroachment and other threats.

Illegal trade and over-exploitation – There is a large trade in snakes and snake products, much of it illegal and often detrimental to local populations. Live snakes are bought and sold for the pet trade and although many of these animals are captive bred, there is also a market for animals from the wild, often rare species that are particularly sought-after by unscrupulous collectors. Snake skins, especially those from various python and boa species and the Oriental rat snake, are used in the production of handbags, shoes and other products. Numbers of skins traded may be high, and tens of thousands of skins of certain species, such as the boa constrictor, may be sold every year. Some snakes are captive bred for the snake-skin trade, but the vast

Marbled tree boa in the Amazon rainforest.

*This diamondback rattlesnake is demonstrating its threat display because
it thinks the photographer is an aggressor. Snakes only attack humans in defense,
so if you encounter one, simply give it some space and let it go on its way.*

majority are from wild populations which, as a result, are sometimes in danger of over-exploitation. Sea snakes are harvested for their skins and for food but they also suffer from being taken as by-catch during fishing operations. Figures from the early 1990s suggested that somewhere in the region of 120,000 sea snakes were taken as by-catch during a single prawn-fishing season off North Queensland, Australia.

Persecution – The fear provoked by snakes, even completely harmless species, can result in high levels of deliberate persecution. In addition to being an animal welfare issue, persecution can also become a conservation issue when local snake populations are put at the risk of extinction.

Persecution is usually *ad hoc* and opportunistic, but probably the most abhorrent displays of organized snake persecution are the annual rattlesnake round-ups which mainly take place in Texas and Oklahoma in the U.S.A.. Round-ups are publicized in spring and hunters can be paid to collect large numbers of animals, often using cruel methods such as forcing them into the open by pouring gasoline into their burrows. There are also organized public round-ups when a lot of wildlife habitat can be destroyed during the search. The captured snakes are kept in holding areas for up to five months, sometimes used in cruel public displays, and eventually killed by decapitation. Their meat may be eaten and skins used in the leather trade. About 270,000–500,000 snakes are killed this way every year.

Discoveries to be Made and Attitudes to Change

A major problem we have is that the impact of these types of threats on snakes is often not well understood since information on their population status is usually lacking. Therefore it can be hard to tell to what extent many species are threatened. There is a lot more to find out about all aspects of the natural history of the 2700 or so snake species. New species continue to be discovered, such as the Vietnamese sharp-nosed snake, for which no live or preserved specimens exist and which is only known from photographs taken by U.S. naval officers in Vietnam in 1968. The original specimens were lost but the photographs provided sufficient details to show that it was a species new to science.

For most snakes, we only know a little or nothing of their ecology since there are probably only a few thousand professional herpetologists (people who study reptiles and amphibians) in the world and only some of them study snakes. Of those that do, a large proportion of work is undertaken on a small number of species which tend to be easier to find and study, such as the garter snakes of North America. This means there is a very important role for the amateur in helping to unlock the secrets of snake natural history through taking part in surveys and collecting valuable ecological information. Budding snake watchers can contact their national herpetological society to find out how they can help and to receive guidance on safe practice.

There are means to counter some of the threats that snakes face, such as designating protected areas, devising and enforcing national and international legislation which provides threatened species with protection from harm and trade, setting quotas on the trade of snakes and snake products and, in extreme cases, developing captive-breeding programmes for species on the edge of extinction. But ultimately none of these will be truly effective until people's attitudes towards snakes change. Conservation of any wildlife species depends, to a large extent, on people's support, and for snakes this is a problem. The human perception of snakes as crafty and evil animals with a mission for death and injury is one that has developed over centuries of ignorance, yet that image still persists today. The reality is that the hundreds of species of snakes are the same as all other animals in that they have evolved over millions of years to fill their ecological niches in their own unique way and with the ultimate aim to reproduce and pass on their genes to their offspring. Humans have been around on earth for only a small fraction of the time that snakes have, so the time has come to get rid of the old prejudices and give them the respect they deserve.

Asian vine snake from the lowland rainforest of Malaysia.

Grass snake.

Table of Snake Families

The scientific and common names of species referred to in the book are listed in their appropriate family.

Family Leptotyphlopidae:
Thread snakes (c. 60 species)
- *Leptotyphlops dulcis*
- *Leptotyphlops occidentalis*
  – Western thread snake

Family Typhlopidae:
Blind snakes (c. 150 species)
- *Rhinotyphlops schegelii* – Giant blind snake

Family Anomalepidae:
(c. 20 species)

Family Uropeltidae:
Shield-tailed snakes and tube snakes (c. 50 species)
Can be divided into 2 sub-families – the
Uropeltinae (shield-tailed snakes) and
Cylindrophinae (tube snakes)

Family Aniliidae:
South American ringed snake (1 species)
- *Anilius scytale*

Family Xenopeltidae:
Sunbeam snake (1 species)
- *Xenopeltis unicolor* – Sunbeam or South
  Asian rainbow snake

Family Loxocemidae:
Mexican dwarf python (1 species)
- *Loxocemus bicolor*

Family Boidae:
Boas and pythons (c. 95 species)
Can be divided into a number of sub-families,
including the Boinae (boas), Erycinae (sand boas)
and Pythoninae (pythons)

- *Boa constrictor* – Boa constrictor (Boinae)
- *Corallus canina* – Emerald tree boa (Boinae)
- *Corallus enydris* – Marbled tree boa (Boinae)
- *Eunectes murinus* – Anaconda (Boinae)
- *Eryx johni* – Sand boa (Erycinae)
- *Aspidites ramsayi* – Woma python (Pythoninae)
- *Chondropython viridis* – Green tree python
  (Pythoninae)
- *Morelia amethystina* – Amethyst python
  (Pythoninae)
- *Morelia bredli* – Bredl's carpet python
  (Pythoninae)
- *Python boeleni* – Boelen's python (Pythoninae)
- *Python molurus* – Indian python (Pythoninae)
- *Python reticulatus* – Reticulated python
  (Pythoninae)